NEW ORLEANS
DECORATIVE IRONWORK

May 24, 1987
For: Marilyn + Leslie —
Finally a visit with you at your home! This is a small reminder of my home! Yours,
Felicia

THE KNAPP PRESS
PUBLISHERS

New Orleans Decorative Ironwork
was created and produced by
REBUS, INC.
and published by THE KNAPP PRESS
5900 Wilshire Boulevard
Los Angeles, California 90036

ISBN 0-89535-156-0

The European and American builders of New Orleans set the city like a stage, striving, perhaps, to turn their difficult terrain—a cypress swamp on the lower Mississippi River—into a dreamy world. That theatrical flair is most conspicuous in ironwork, a structural and ornamental element of the city's eighteenth- and nineteenth-century architecture. Wrought iron and cast iron grace other Southern cities—Charleston and Savannah, particularly—but they virtually define New Orleans and unite the Vieux Carré (the French Quarter) and the American Garden District. Even newcomers are struck by the abundance of the decoration: everywhere there are window grilles, gates, entire verandas of iron.

Graceful spirals of iron brace balconies, which are themselves skirted in metal sculpture. The patterns in the ironwork are all organic and geometric exuberance: morning glories, oak leaves and acorns, fruits, vines;

circles overlap one another within Gothic arches. Cornstalks of iron—in bloom—stand in rows to make distinctive fences. Courtyard and garden furniture—chairs and tables that are nothing but fabulous tangles of steely vines—sit beside iron fountains, attended by iron cherubs and birds. Doorways become grand entrances with the right iron flourishes—custom hinges, knockers and bells, carriage lamps, transoms, outer gates of iron trelliswork. In New Orleans even hardware details are prettier than they need be: rivets are not simply rivets but rosettes, sunbursts, fleurs-de-lis. This sculptural splendor is the obvious appeal of iron, though the medium has the compelling quality, too, of melding opposites—it is simultaneously strong and delicate, light and heavy, masculine and feminine. "Iron lace," the immortal metaphor, fairly swathes New Orleans and draws us into its veil.

The earliest ironwork in New Orleans was

wrought by hand, some of it shipped from Spain. Locally wrought iron, from the late eighteenth century, is as fine as that of the European masters. "Blacksmiths" does not adequately describe those who produced it, for they were artists at anvils, really; in New Orleans most of these men were blacks, Germans, and Irishmen. Working in broad strokes, they hammered hot slugs of iron into elaborate scrolls, then joined them into brackets, gates, window grilles, and various decorative pieces. Distinct from cast iron—a later variety—wrought iron looks, as it is, handmade: wonderfully plastic, it seems to have not quite hardened. Its licorice-like quality is all in the making, for when heated and hammered the metal is not only rendered pliable but is rid of most impurities. Wrought iron will not rust, and it takes a high polish.

By the mid-nineteenth century decorative cast iron was being created in foundries originally set up to produce heavy sugar-milling equipment, and industry and art flourished together. In the foundry process molten metal was poured into wooden molds carved in extravagant patterns—leaves, flowers, vines, abstracts. Cast iron, not wrought iron, is the lacy variety, and its frilliness was a fine match for the decorative essentials of the Victorian period: rococo furnishings, floral carpets, lace curtains, classical sculpture, florid wallpapers and window shades.

Since it is not forged but simply poured, cast iron is not as pure as wrought iron—it tends to be brittle and lacks luster. Its high carbon content inevitably caused rust, and New Orleanians painted the iron, often a cool sea-green—a protective measure that also added to the general ornament. Architectural elements of iron were a much safer bet than wood in the humid city—most of the Corinthian and Ionic columns on the Garden District's Greek Revival mansions were cast of iron and painted white. Architectural ironwork could have a protective function as well, for spiked balcony railings and fences discouraged, or punished, intruders.

New Orleanians were not restricted to local work, as fine as it was. There were occasional imports of European wrought iron, and there were shipments of cast iron from New York and Philadelphia. Wood & Perot, an important Philadelphia firm with a New Orleans outlet, listed in its catalog over 250 patterns of balcony railings and fences: albeit bulky, they could be ordered like any other mail-order merchandise.

People of the most discriminating tastes (and the financial means) did not shop the catalogs but commissioned their own cast-iron designs. Such custom work might feature family crests, personal mascots, any favorite motif or image—hearts, stars, animals, cherubs. One apparently eager father chose the medium of cast iron to announce his daughter's availability to suitors, for he filled the balcony railings outside her bedroom with cupids and arrows. Monograms could also be cast in iron, and to have one's initials intertwined in an already florid balcony railing or gate was surely the most elegant homeowner signature.

This is a city where people even took ironwork to their graves, in cast-iron tombs and graveyard statuary. Fences surrounding New Orleans' old cemeteries are often of iron, and their gates bear angels, lambs, and weeping willows—cast in iron for eternity.

A PORTFOLIO OF
NEW ORLEANS DECORATIVE IRONWORK

The rear gate of the Ursuline convent, built in the late 1740s, bears what are perhaps among the oldest wrought-iron ornaments in the entire Mississippi River valley. The grille beneath the cross affords a peek at the convent's vast parterre gardens.

1

Graceful wrought iron rails a balcony of the Ca-bildo, the Spanish government house on Jackson Square. The ensemble is exquisite: the French doors and fanlight, the sun's reflection on the glass panes, and, especially, the masterfully wrought iron. The cartouchelike railing is the work of Marcellino Her-nandez, a Canary Islander who created most of the ironwork for the Cabildo in the 1790s.

Marcellino Hernandez fashioned this unique balcony railing in 1795 for the Chartres Street house of a Spaniard named Bartholeme Bosque: the artist wove his client's initials into the baroque scrollwork. Hernandez captured all the richness of wrought iron, as if it were still warm and pliable.

As if growing on their own trellis, grapevines crawl up and about the front of a shuttered brick house in the French Quarter. The arbor—really a veranda overlooking the street—is of silvery cast iron.

Clutching a little wreath, a nymph romps around the balcony of a mansion built in 1856 by one of New Orleans' great merchants. The old Daily Crescent, *reviewing that year's architectural commissions, praised the French Quarter home as the city's "finest residence downtown." Each nymph in the balcony railing is framed in small circles and appears amid a tangle of grapevines—a tantalizing suggestion of bacchanalian revelry.*

This magnificent cast-iron gate, framed by Corinthian columns, protects the entrance of Gallier House, which architect James Gallier, Jr. built as his family's private residence in 1857. A refreshing green, the gate could remain closed with the front door open: on hot summer days the family enjoyed any cooling breezes while maintaining their security.

A loopy A and P—*entwined along the cast-iron balcony railings of the twin Pontalba buildings facing Jackson Square—form the elegant monogram of the woman who built the row houses, Baroness Micaela Almonester de Pontalba. The Pontalba railings are among the most ornate—and are certainly the longest—in the city.*

Flowering iron vines cast their shadows inside a shady veranda—a cool summer retreat. The frilly ironwork is at home here, even on a stately exterior.

The ornament on this iron fence is spare, but its message is clear: the anvil, hammer, and tongs mark the site of an 1864 ironworks. At this city foundry local artisans—using the tools represented here— wrought some of New Orleans' finest ironwork.

9

The severe vertical lines of a French Quarter fence, here in detail, are relieved by a rich floral pattern in its gate. A cool green, and all fruits and flowers, the gate offers a glimpse into the lush courtyard it protects.

10

A scrim of white cast iron turns this grand house into a summer pavilion—the lacy, arched framework of iron is cool to look at, cool to the touch. Palmetto fans and spears alternate in the fence surrounding the property.

An iron lamp, framed in steely curls, hangs from an elaborately wrought brace. When aglow the lamp marks an elegant evening entrance.

The cast iron so abundant on the facade of this Garden District house has an organic quality—its tendrils are almost indistinguishable from the twisted tree branches in the foreground. The fence, columns, and balcony railings bring a romantic touch to the formal, arched doorway.

What is surely New Orleans' most exuberant, and famous, cast-iron fence—stalks of corn, seemingly ready to harvest—surrounds an Italianate villa in the Garden District.

Spring azaleas mingle with iron ears of corn in this detail from the cornstalk fence. There are only two such fences in the city; the other is on Royal Street in the French Quarter.

CREDITS

All photography by Karen Radkai except cover and numbers 2, 7, 14, and 15 by Paul Rocheleau

Picture Editor: Mary Z. Jenkins; Editor: Vance Muse; Designer: Ronald Gross; Production: Paul Levin; Managing Editor: Fredrica Harvey